LIGHT AT THE
TUNNEL'S END

Light at the Tunnel's End

The Struggle to Overcome Prostate Cancer

BY JOHN HEILMANN

SERENDIPITY

Copyright © John Heilmann, 2003

First published in 2003 by
Serendipity
Suite 530
37 Store Street
Bloomsbury
London

British Library Cataloguing-in-Publication data
A record for this book is available from the British Library

ISBN 1 84394 055 8

Printed and bound by Bookcraft Ltd, Bath

Contents

This book is dedicated:

To my wife, my children and grandchildren, who steadfastly gave their encouragement and support to my efforts to combat this disease.

To the professors, physicians, researchers, nurses and support staffs of the University of Virginia Health Services, who together are succeeding in their quest to cure and eradicate cancer.

To all prostate cancer specialists the world over who are striving to rid humanity of this dread disease.

Particular thanks go to the teaching physicians of the University of Virginia, who supported and advised me in this writing endeavour.

Professor William D. Steer, MD, FACS, Chaiman, Department of Urology.

Professor Tyvin Rich, MD, FACR, Department of Radiation Oncology.

Professor Jay Y. Gillenwater, MD, Department of Urology.

Prologue

Nobody ever expects to receive a call from a family member telling you that they have cancer. It's something that happens to other people, but not to you. At first I was in shock, and that sinking, nauseating feeling came over me. I quickly moved into denial: *Perhaps the test results were someone else's. But if not, is it curable? What kind of cancer is it? What are the repercussions? Was it caught in time? If so, what will the side effects be?*

These are all questions that went through my mind. I quickly determined that having the answers to these questions and all the options outlined was going to be the most urgent and important part in solving the angst and fear we all shared.

Inevitably and unfortunately, there are doctors out there who have no compassion or tact whilst sentencing you 'to the grave'. A cold 50/50 chance and two options are all you are afforded, with no hope of anything positive. This is where a second or third opinion becomes crucial. As in the cases of myself and my dad, finding the right doctor made a huge difference to our recuperation and peace of mind. Understanding techniques, side effects, medication, diet and psychological ramifications, all play an important part in recovery ... as knowledge is power.

As a family we are extremely fortunate and blessed, as things were caught in the early stages. In many cases, it's denial that allows these things to go too far. Knowing that something is wrong and not doing anything about it only diminishes your chances of beating it. But living without my parents is not an option.

Suzanne Heilmann

The foregoing sentiments were expressed by my daughter, in reaction to being informed of my diagnosis of prostate cancer. She has herself been successfully treated for facial skin cancer, and therefore has a special insight on the experience of coping with the disease in one of its multiple manifestations. She, along with the other members of my family, has urged and supported the writing of this book in an effort to help other cancer sufferers understand and cope with the disease. This book is dedicated to my family, with heartfelt gratitude for the love and support each member has given me through this ordeal.

John Heilmann

Introduction

There is a great wealth of documented information available on the subject of cancer. Scientific papers are exchanged within the medical profession, and a great number are published in professional journals of medicine. But for the most part, this information is lodged in the halls of academia, and not easily available to individual access. The purpose of this book is to provide the lay reader with the practical knowledge of how one prostate cancer victim experienced the process of treatment, from diagnosis to recovery. It should be borne in mind that this is a single patient's experience. It will be informative in that respect, but this book should not be construed as a blueprint for general assumptions, nor specific applications.

In most large bookstores, one will find an entire bookcase devoted to the memoirs of women who have been afflicted with breast cancer. The literature available for men who have to cope with prostate cancer, however, usually occupies only, at best, a half-shelf. My hope is that this book will help to expand that half-shelf, as it were, to give the reading public and the prostate cancer victims, with their families, one more memoir from which to draw critical knowledge, and to expand the empathy (and sympathy) for one of society's least understood, yet most widely spread, diseases.

In other words, I wish to help the reader understand the disease and what to do about it, with the best available professional medical guidance. It will also address the pertinent factors relating to expected quality of life after the successful completion of a particular course of treatment.

I

It was a sultry, late May Friday, the precursor of another boiling Virginia summer inevitably on its way. It was also the beginning of Memorial Day Weekend, but most importantly to me, the day my urologist was supposed to convey the results of the prostate biopsy, when received from the pathological examiners.

The anxiety of awaiting these results was of course a mental burden. To alleviate the pressure, I decided to go outdoors and work, sweat and all, on jobs that needed attention in the yard. It was my way of keeping in motion, concentrating on specific trimming or weeding goals. This was an excuse to remain active and push aside the cloud of concern about the anticipated biopsy result. It was a mind-over-matter, or push-aside, attitude, underpinned by the anxiety of awaiting a crucial, perhaps life-altering, medical assessment of my health, well-being and longevity. Despite the concentration on my yard work, my thoughts oscillated like a swinging pendulum, between the extremes of having no problem at all, and the prospect of the presence of cancer.

I went into the house to get a drink of water. I was about to return outside when the phone rang. It was the urologist's office. The anxiously awaited call!

'Mr Heilmann, Dr Carter has asked me to call and give you the results of your biopsy, which we received today from the pathology lab. Unfortunately, they are positive. You have cancer of the prostate.'

'Would you please repeat that?' I asked; which the nurse did.

'Could you inform me, please, of the extent of the cancer presence?'

'I cannot give you any further details at this time. Dr Carter has all the information in the pathologist's analysis.'

'May I please speak with the doctor, then?'

'I am sorry. Dr Carter has left the clinic for the weekend. He requests that you come in Tuesday afternoon at 3:30 p.m. for an appointment. May I put you down on his schedule for that time?'

'Yes, of course. I'll be there. Is there any way I can speak to Dr Carter before Tuesday? Where could I reach him?'

'I'm sorry, Mr Heilmann. He is out of town through the Memorial Day holiday.'

So began a long, bleak weekend. So also began the critical quest for information and knowledge about prostate cancer. I sprang into a process of searching out information on the best available means of combating this insidious disease. However, the first hurdle to overcome was three long, dark days of anxiety and pressure, not knowing the extent or seriousness of my problem. It would be a tormenting seventy-two hours of mental anguish and emotional stress. As a healthy, active individual with good annual medical checkup results—and one proud of the results—it was a dramatic hit to the ego. *What, me?! I don't believe it!*

My wife Inge-Marie, who had heard the dialogue with Dr Carter's nurse on the speaker phone, was at first silently stunned. *My healthy, energetic husband has cancer?*

She and I fell into an abjectly reflective mood, with few words exchanged. As the news sank in, we kept our hands busy, tidying up in the kitchen. Our minds variously raced through a myriad of possible consequences. The problem was, we did not know the extent of the cancer, nor did we yet have any real knowledge of the available methods of treatment, nor of their success rates. We were left in the dark, with our fears bouncing back and forth between imagined dire consequences and optimistic hope that the situation would be totally surmountable.

That weekend we combated a plethora of emotions, bouncing between anger and self-directed compassion, pessimism and optimism. All thought was speculation, for we were in the dark, with no facts yet in our possession. As a retired business executive, I was imbued with the process of disciplined decision-making, based on the available data. The frustration of trying to decide something without the necessary knowledge was excruciating.

I was a healthy, active person, living life to the full, with no symptoms and no abnormalities. Annual medical checkups had revealed only a gradual, slight enlarging of the prostate gland—a common, mostly benign characteristic of men in their fifties and beyond. Thoughts that occurred to me over and over again that weekend were: *What is happening to me? Is this the start on a path which will seriously affect my longevity? What on earth should I do? Where do I find the solution to this problem?* Or even more macabre: *Is this the beginning of a death march?*

My emotions and intellect became united toward a self-imposed cold calm. The greatest fear that can beset a person is the fear of the unknown. My resolve was to get myself educated about my problem, however vaguely defined. I grabbed every opportunity to learn about the disease and its consequences. I read and researched a lot that weekend, and created an enormous list of questions. I also spoke with a close friend who himself had overcome prostate cancer. He had decided on Radical Prostatectomy (surgery to remove the prostate gland), and in his words, 'It was certainly an ordeal, but worth it, because the final outcome was successful.' Knowing him as a friend for many years, I considered him now to be in good health, as he expressed he was. He distantly exhibited contentment with the quality of his life, now restored, many months after the surgery.

So the miserable weekend wore on, through Memorial Day, inching onward, minute by minute. The television, especially the sports programs, provided some diversion from my research activity. After a less than restful Monday night, and a routine morning schedule of work on our property, it was time to leave for my appointment with Dr Carter. I arrived at the clinic twenty minutes early, primarily because of my anxiety. Fifteen minutes beyond the time of the appointment, sitting in the public lounge, my name was called. I eagerly followed the nurse assistant to a coldly clinical cubicle which was dominated by an examination table and numerous medical apparatuses. There I was asked to await the doctor. Alone.

I was left in a high state of emotional tension for forty minutes. Finally, my urologist came through the door, carrying a folder with a sheaf of papers in it. An abrupt, formal greeting of 'Hello again, Mr Heilmann' was responded to by my anxious 'Hello, doctor.' The dialogue was henceforth strictly clinical. He described the extent of the cancer cell count arising from the biopsy results. It showed a relatively low percentage of malignant cells, when related to the whole count of all the cells of the prostate specimens taken.

Conclusion: 'You have cancer of the prostate, but it is not widespread in the gland. However, you have cancerous cells, which must be eradicated to prevent spread.'

I knew already that my blood work analysis showed a PSA* of 7. The PSA number is the critical, first-level

---

* *Prostate Specific Antigen* is a substance produced solely by the prostate gland. A PSA test measures the level of this substance in the bloodstream. Very little PSA escapes from a healthy prostate into the bloodstream, but certain abnormal conditions, particularly cancerous activity, can cause larger amounts of PSA to be emitted into the blood. Hence, a higher level of PSA measurement may signal the presence of prostate cancer. A reading of over 6 is considered to be a warning signal of a malignant tumor presence. My PSA results demonstrated a factor 7!

measurement of the presence of prostate cancer. It is a barometric reading of your prostate's health. A PSA reading should be a standard ingredient of the annual physical checkup for any male fifty and older. A further reason my physician had suspected the possibility of cancer was from my DRE,* another standard part of an older male's annual physical. This involves an examination via the rectum, in which it is possible to literally *feel* for a tumor.

The doctor informed me that, while the malignant cell count revealed by the biopsy was not high, the threat of spread to other areas and organs was serious, and I should contemplate fairly prompt action to remedy the problem. The question was: *Which course of remedial action should be taken?* I felt that Dr Carter, a urological surgeon himself, was overly strong in recommending radical surgery, but he did say there were other courses of action available. He continued to reiterate that the 'cleanest and clearest' course

---

* A *Digital Rectal Exam* (or DRE) is a simple test in which the doctor inserts a lubricated, gloved finger into the rectum and feels the prostate for signs of abnormal size and shape. Should the doctor detect something abnormal or suspicious, he will refer to the PSA number. If the combination of the DRE and PSA further the suspicions of prostate cancer, you will be advised to see a urologist for an examination, which should include a biopsy of the prostate.

Such a biopsy involves the removal of very small amounts of tissue from the prostate, through hollow needles inserted via the rectum. *Transrectal Ultrasonography* (TRUS) is used to guide the needle placement during this process. TRUS employs high frequency sound waves to create a visual image of the prostate on a video monitor. There is little or no pain involved; only mild discomfort, at worst. Because biopsies are invasive procedures, some short-term side effects, such as infection and minor rectal bleeding, can occur. But serious complications are very rare. (Antibiotics are prescribed, however, as a preventive measure.)

The removed tissue is submitted to a pathologist's microscope to ascertain whether cancer cells are present. Only upon completion of a biopsy can the presence of prostate cancer be confirmed definitely.

was to submit myself to Radical Prostatectomy, which equated to 'cutting it all out'.

I was given a paperback, *Prostate Cancer and its Possible Cures*, a somewhat dramatic, tabloid-like publication. (While providing basic information on prostate cancer procedures, it sensationalized its content with stories of luminaries who had or had not survived after treatment. The effect was to raise fears on the one hand, while abating them on the other, by glorifying the successful results.) I was urged to read the book and advise him within ten days of my decision of what course to follow. A few more general questions and answers, together with the offer of the name of an oncologist close to his practice, resulted in a brief salutation of departure from the encounter, leaving me only further bewildered and anxious to seek and find the right course of treatment to follow.

I was grateful that the results showed clear containment of the cancer without spread. However, I felt dissatisfied, insecure and unhappy with this immediate experience. Consequently, I decided to obtain a second opinion, biopsy and all. I called my internist. He had also received the biopsy results from the pathologist's laboratory, so he knew of the results. He advised me to accept the pathological conclusion. I stated that, as a surgeon, the urologist seemed much too keen to cut. I added that before going forward, I needed other expert opinions on what my alternatives might be. My own research was beginning to indicate that radical surgery was statistically proven, over time, to have the leading success rate. With surgery, however, the subsequent permanent negative effects on my quality of life were likely to be severe, compared to some of the other remedies. Realizing my need for more information, I decided to examine all aspects and alternative remedies extensively. Pivotal to my ultimate determination would be the cure which would least affect the quality of my active lifestyle.

My internist agreed with my thinking, and suggested that I call Professor William Steers, at the University of Virginia Health Sciences Center in Charlottesville, to obtain a second opinion, plus advice on what to do. That was the course I opted to follow. I immediately phoned Professor Steers' office, and explained to his secretary why I was calling. With great fortune, I was given a morning appointment in his office at the UVA Medical Services Center of Urology and Radiation the very next day.

Driving up, alone in my car, I pondered the aspects of my diagnosed condition. It was a beautiful spring day. As I cruised through the mountainous areas between my country home and Charlottesville, I contemplated my joy in living life. The winding highway through the Blue Ridge Mountains, the tree-clad hills and valleys—so exquisitely beautiful, bathed in the early morning sun rays, patches of mist in the inner valleys, rising to meet the day. I drew in with enjoyment the beauty I was beholding. The spoiling intrusion was: *How long was it going to last?* I resolved to enjoy each day on its own, and face tomorrow as it appeared. And deep from my soul welled up a phrase that would become my mantra throughout my recovery:

I AM GOING TO BEAT THIS!

I pulled into the hospital parking lot, parked my car and wended my way through a labyrinth of corridors to the Urology Department. I announced myself at the reception desk, and was told Professor Steers would be with me shortly. Waiting room, magazines, observation of congregated patients, waiting phlegmatically for their turn. Soon a white uniformed nurse appeared through the door, asking for a Mr Heilmann. Remembering the rather cold, formal, first meeting with the urologist, I thought: *Here I go again!* But Professor Steers' reception and greeting were quite gracious, with little formality. Despite my concerns, I felt guardedly

9

comfortable. I sensed that I might be entrusting myself to the right hands. This *felt* like the right person to give me critical advice and a solution to my problem!

We chatted, somewhat nonchalantly, as he revisited the clinical information which he had received. I watched him ponder the statistics. He was a handsome man in his forties, with dark brown hair, loosely kempt, and deep-set brown eyes in a fine-featured face. He concentrated silently on the job at hand.

Finally, a slight warm smile appeared. 'Mr Heilmann, it is clear that you have the problem of a cancerous growth on your prostate gland. But I need more information before I can confirm its extent and seriousness. I need the slides of the biopsy cells for a recheck and confirmation of the pathologist's report—which I would request you to obtain and have sent to us here. With this additional information, our people can conclude the correctness of the diagnosis up to this point. Please take immediate steps to have these elements of the puzzle forwarded to me, and I will follow up.'

The compassionate, yet entirely professional, approach to my condition was in itself a huge relief. This confirmed my feeling that I had been directed into the right hands. My spirits were already rising. My natural inclination toward optimism was perhaps being rewarded. But a voice in my mind cautioned: *Let us see.*

What followed was a dialogue, mostly one-sided from Professor Steers, who went into great detail in addressing the treatment options that were available, the protocol that each entailed, and their statistical success rates. Key to the last would lie in the careful and correct diagnostic conclusions drawn from further examinations of the patient. It became evident that, subject to these findings, I would personally make the decisions as to the choice of treatment to be followed absent the discovery of an advanced state of cancerous spread, in which case, certain protocols would be virtually mandated by the doctors. This was a determination yet to be made.

Professor Steers took a few relaxed moments to chat personally with me. It was a warm, charming interlude, during which I felt we were beginning to get to know each other. The conversation was human, concerned and amicable. It enveloped topics of our sentiments, thus our personal lives. It was wonderful. But most important, I felt I had found the best possible physician for the job.

II

As I soon discovered from my own research, and from the conversation with Dr Steers, the options available were numerous, but boiled down to two major courses of action, in combination with various supportive means of treatment: Surgery or Radiation. The supportive treatments presented a variety of means to back these up. What follows is an explanation of what the primary actions are, as well as a classification of secondary or support actions that might be taken. All will depend on the diagnostic evaluation of the seriousness of the overall situation, which boils down to whether the cancer is contained or has spread beyond the prostate gland.

With the courtesy of the Mayo Clinic Health Center newsletter of October 2000 and the University of Virginia medical team, these are the decision-making alternatives available to prostate cancer patients. It should be understood that there are certain critical factors that play a role in the selection of the appropriate procedure. These are, *First:* How early was the diagnosis of cancer clinically revealed? *Second:* How fast is the tumor growing, and therefore, how much has it spread? *Third:* What is your general state of health? And *Finally:* What is your age? With these established facts in mind, you and your physician should review all the available alternative procedures.

1. **Watchful Waiting.** This treatment is fairly straightforward. Specifically, it entails close scrutiny of new signs or symptoms that may appear, indicating any need for action.

In order to be watchful, while waiting, regular blood tests and rectal examinations are required to track the status of the cancer. Your physician will also likely perform occasional biopsies.

This option is often recommended for men aged seventy or older, when the cancer tumor is small, contained and growing slowly. At such a greater age, statistics show that when the cancer growth is slow, and the spread low-paced, the possible course of serious problems is limited. This approach is particularly prominent in Scandinavian countries, based on research done in that part of the world particularly, but also elsewhere. The point is: life expectancy for such a patient may be good and longer by not doing anything invasive or involving radiation treatment. The stress of invasive or radiological treatment could actually create more risks than the slow-growing cancer poses.

The objective of Watchful Waiting is, therefore, to balance the growth and spread prognosis with the strains and pressures of critical treatment, for a positive end result. You have the fallback position, at any given time, depending on periodic test results, of invoking a more aggressive approach and action, if necessary.

Your physician may not recommend Watchful Waiting if you are younger and in good health. The reason for this is time-based: as your life expectancy is longer, your cancer will have that much more time to grow. And the malignant cells would have a greater opportunity to spread, possibly becoming unexpectedly aggressive, making cure less likely.

As someone very near seventy years, in otherwise good health, I decided that I was not going to wait—whatever the arguments might be for doing so. My position was: if it is there, it should be eradicated. I desired to be psychologically and physiologically as healthy as before. I discarded the idea of Watchful Waiting, and proceeded to examine the active remedial procedures available. Hence, I went with the expert advice of the University of Virginia Medical Services group.

2. Surgery. Radical Prostatectomy is considered the most effective way of curing cancer confined to the prostate gland: that is, removing the prostate gland entirely. A radical procedure indeed! While the surgical techniques for its implementation continue to become more and more refined, this type of surgery has had drastic consequences for most men, who become either impotent or have greatly reduced sexual function. Likewise, many bladder problems can occur, including incontinence.

These surgical procedures fortunately continue to improve steadily. New techniques allow for the removal of the prostate in ways that minimize the damage to muscles and nerves that control urination and sexual function. Because of these improvements, the number of men who choose to have radical surgery performed has reached 25 per cent; whereas, a decade ago, only 10 per cent resorted to surgery.

The most commonly followed prostate removal procedure is called *Retropubic Surgery*. Here, the prostate is removed through an incision in the lower abdomen. The surgeon may also remove some lymph nodes located near the gland and send them for pathological analysis to determine if cancer is present. As the lymph nodes are in close proximity to the prostate itself, they are easy candidates for the spread of the cancer. If they indeed are cancerous, the surgeon will decide whether to proceed with the surgery or to leave the gland in place. This decision will be based on the number of lymph nodes showing evidence of cancer, one's age and any other symptoms. The fewer nodes with cancer, the younger one is, and the fewer symptoms there are, the more likely it will be that the surgery will be continued to comprehensive completion. The logic of this decision is based on the higher degree of success the state of the disease presents for cure.

After the prostate gland is removed, the surgeon will reconstruct part of the bladder. This may involve attaching the urethra and the sphincter muscle directly to the bladder. The sphincter controls the flow of urine from the bladder. This surgical attachment is done to increase the chances of regaining such flow control. It should be noted, however, that achieving bladder control again, even with this procedure, may take weeks, months or even longer. About 95 per cent of men eventually do regain complete bladder control. Most of the remainder experience 'stress incontinence', which means urine escapes when the bladder is pressured suddenly, by acts such as coughing, sneezing, laughing or lifting.

The surgeon will also try to save the nerve bundles located on each side of the prostate gland. These nerve bundles control the ability to have an erection. One or both bundles are often saved. Men in their forties and fifties who opt for this nerve sparing surgery are more likely to retain their ability to have an erection. Between 60 and 80 per cent of men younger than fifty who have this type of surgery are able to achieve normal erections afterward. Only 15 to 20 per cent of men in their sixties and seventies return to normal sexual activity.

There is another form of surgical incursion which is used in the process of curing prostate cancer called *Perineal Surgery*. Today, it is less commonly used. It involves making an incision between the anus and the scrotal sac. However, this procedure encumbers the surgeon's ability to locate and save the nerve bundles. Likewise, the surgeon will not be able to reach the nearby lymph nodes, should they be cancerous. Hence, this procedure is relatively ineffective and on the way out. But one must be aware enough to ask the prospective surgeon which specific procedure is recommended, and why, in order to be forewarned of its effectiveness for one's specific case.

There is a surgical procedure that needs mentioning although it is resorted to with less frequency as other treatment alternatives gain in application and resultant success. It is called Bilateral Orchiectomy, which is the name given to the removal of the testicles in order to halt, or certainly greatly diminish, production of the male hormone testosterone. This hormone, as will be discussed when other treatments are described, has been found to contribute to the growth of cancer cells in the prostate gland.

The operation can be done on an outpatient basis; however, hospitalisation for two to three days is more commonly desired. It is carried out with the use of both general and local anesthesia, a choice most frequently left to the patient. Because the scrotum, in which the incisions for removal are made, contains relatively few pain fibres, discomfort from the surgery is at a low level and healing is fairly rapid. Bilateral Orchiectomy, while resorted to less and less, does have some serious side effects and complications which should be noted, as follows:

- It cannot be reversed.
- Most men suffer psychologically because of the removal of the testes, causing impotence.
- Breast tenderness and swelling occur fairly frequently.
- Recurring hot flushes are common.

While this may be regarded as a less utilised surgical procedure, it is nevertheless one of which a patient should be aware.

3. Radiation. As research and consequent improvements in technology progress, the success of radiation in curing prostate cancer is growing. Radiation is now an effective alternative to surgery, and may be the preferred treatment for many reasons, especially if one's specific condition may include having a difficult time tolerating surgery. More importantly, it may provide the exact same cure results as surgery, but with fewer side- or after-effects. While inconvenient to many body functions, it is relatively painless throughout its duration. The effectiveness rate, if the cancer is confined to the prostate, is equal to that of surgery for at least ten years, according to currently available statistics. However, radiation is also used to treat cancer that has spread outside the prostate, with a high level of success.

The principal radiation delivery methods available are:

External Beam Therapy. This is the most commonly used method. It entails the use of an X-ray beam, produced by a machine that precisely focuses radiation on the cancerous tissues in question. A form of therapy called *three-dimensional conformal action* focuses the radiation dose precisely to the affected area, while minimizing the exposure to normal, healthy tissues. The actual treatment process takes only minutes per application, including preparation time. The applications are generally given five days a week for a continuous period of five to eight weeks. (An experimental form of External Beam Therapy uses protons in place of X-rays to kill cancer cells. Protons travel through non-cancerous tissues and come to rest in the targeted area, where the radiation dose is deposited. How this treatment compares to that of X-rays is not yet entirely known.)

External Beam Radiation therapy may cause side effects during and after the treatment process, including impaired sexual function, diarrhea, rectal bleeding, a burning sensation around the rectal area, and the persistent feeling of needing a bowel movement. More urgent and frequent urination may also occur. The good news is that these problems usually subside once treatments end.

The second of the principal radiation processes is *Implantation of Radioactive Seed.* (The clinical name for it is

Brachytherapy.) This type of radiation involves implanting tiny radioactive seeds into the prostate. The one-time surgical procedure takes between one and two hours, and may be done under full anesthesia, or with local anesthetic application. Hollow needles, guided by an ultrasound unit, are inserted into the gland, and the seeds are expelled into their target areas where they stay, emitting radiation which destroys the cancer. It is believed that the resulting effect does not escape from the prostate area, but doctors recommend that any patient carrying these seeds stay at least six feet away from children or pregnant women for a minimum of two months after the procedure. This is simply a safety precaution.

Seed implantation is relatively new and its long-term effects are not yet fully available. However, short-term successes suggest that this may become a more common form of prostate cancer treatment in the coming years. Early studies indicate that the seeds control cancer growth for five years in 90 per cent of men, and for ten years in 85 per cent of men. Impotence is believed to occur in 1 out of 6 patients, compared with 1 in 2 when Beam Radiation alone is used. Incontinence or rectal function problems are uncommon.

4. Cryotherapy. Yet another non-surgical treatment of prostate cancer is in its developmental stages, without, as yet, enough conclusive results. It is called *Cryotherapy*, which is a freezing process applied to the gland's cancerous area. The procedure involves inserting five to seven thin metal rods through the perineum (the area between the scrotum and the anus) and into the prostate. Liquid nitrogen is circulated through the rods, dropping the local temperature in the affected area to −374° Fahrenheit. Freezing the cancer cells causes them to rupture and expire—at least that is the theory of the process. But full annihilation of the malignant cells does not always occur, and frequent repetition becomes necessary. Furthermore, results show impotence is a permanent after-effect in 80 per cent of the men treated, and thus far, long-term survival rates are lower than with surgery or radiation. This potential remedy has a long way to go before it is accepted as a reliable cure.

In closing this passage on available alternatives for cure, it should be said that scientific research and development is being undertaken on many fronts. Studies in genetics and genetic engineering, along with immune system science, which includes development of specific vaccines, and a host of pharmacological remedies, are being pursued worldwide. Mankind's ingenuity and ability to create technology based on scientific research is well on the way to defeating the cancer disease in whatever form. The success rates in fighting this insidious disease are already manifest. Beating cancer is a goal which we all have, and as survival rates become increasingly positive, optimism and personal resolve are essential ingredients for success, victim or not!

An interesting aside: when I told a physician friend that my prostate cancer diagnosis was positive, he responded sympathetically, but optimistically, and said that prostate cancer is for men what breast cancer is for women: unfortunately too common to both genders. The outlook, however, is hugely positive. For cancer treatments have come so far that a cancer diagnosis no longer means an immediate death sentence.

III

It was now decision time. Having researched and educated myself as best I could, it was time to return to Professor Steers and address the question of what avenue to go down, based on the knowledge available and now understood. So an appointment with the professor was sought and made. In the intervening time, while I was reading up on available procedures, the professor was also studying his options, based on the medical records I had sent him. My dossier now known to him, he proclaimed me otherwise healthy and in a positive position to move forward.

Once again, I found the professor warm and courteous, at the same time utterly professional in his demeanor. After some general questions about how I was feeling physically and mentally, the dialogue turned to what course of action should be taken. Much of what was discussed, with the doctor leading the conversation, never balking at my questions, took me through the various protocols (covered in the previous chapter), describing all the options available for choice.

Professor Steers suggested that I might want to take a little time, a week or so, to think through the alternatives and then make my decision known in a follow-up meeting. I was calm and confident that all my research, combined with his answers to my queries and questions, had equipped me with the necessary facts to make my decision. He was very clear on a single important point, which was that he would provide complete disclosure of the procedural options available, *but the final decision was to be mine,* not one forced upon me by him.

I took the bull by the horns right then and there, and said that my mind was made up. I told him that with what I had learned, and with his answers to my questions in this meeting, my decision was to proceed with the radiation protocol. There was a moment of quiet during which a small smile appeared on Dr Steers' face, followed by the comment that he had hoped this would be my decision. He endorsed it heartily. He said that, had I been of younger age, of poorer general health, and had the cancer been advanced or spread, he would personally have recommended an immediate surgical incursion. He added, 'I would have had you on the operating table within days.' This fortunately was not the case.

Such a positive endorsement from such a highly esteemed professional medic gave a huge sense of relief. I was almost joyful, despite the anxiety of wondering if all of this, when implemented as a medical protocol, would actually work and become a cure.

With this important decision taken, and with a relatively high degree of comfort, the next thing was to get on with it. My mind was made up. I convinced myself that I had the best team available in the country to work with in fulfilling my goal. I repeated to myself again: *'I'M GOING TO BEAT THIS!'*

My team of physicians and professors worked at the University of Virginia Health Services Center, in the Departments of Urology and Radiation Oncology. Professor Steers was at the head of the Center, while two other professors, Dr Gillenwater and Dr Rich, headed Urology and Radiation Oncology respectively. My first appointments were made with these two doctors, and several days later I returned to meet with them.

After completion of all the obligatory paperwork to register as a patient, I was ready to see Dr Gillenwater, and was soon accompanied to his office by a nurse assistant. I found myself in a windowless study. The white walls were covered with framed diplomas, and the bookshelves filled with medical books and journals. There was an orderly, paper-filled desk, with a swivel chair for the doctor and two leather-cushioned chairs facing the desk. I seated myself and awaited his arrival.

Soon a slight man with a balding head ringed by white hair, wearing the customary white medical coat, breezed through the door. He greeted me by name with a smile and a cheerful hello. After a brief question and answer session about my health through the years, he concluded that I was in very good shape for my age, only months away from my seventieth birthday.

While conversing, he was flipping through what was obviously my medical history file. He pointed out that the prostate biopsy results showed a grouping of malignant cell growth on one side of the prostate gland. This he felt was a positive sign, in terms of treatment planning, for it indicated there was a good degree of containment so far. By cancer growth standards, it had been diagnosed at an early stage. The Gleason Score of 5 indicated a moderate level of aggression. Having never heard of a Gleason Score, I was immediately curious and asked for an explanation, which was provided.*

My anxiety was abating a little with such positive comments. He then addressed the chosen course of treatment. He pointed out that the protocol for Brachytherapy was not limited solely

* A Gleason Score is a measure of the grade of a cancerous tumor in the prostate. Grade is the term for the 'aggression level', meaning how quickly it is likely to grow and spread. Pathologists who arrive at a Gleason number are specialists in the interpretation of changes in body tissues caused by the cancer. Their grade of the tumor will be determined by cell appearance, as seen under microscopic examination. Gleason scores denoting aggression levels range from 2 to 10. A score of under 4 indicates low aggressiveness, while 5 to 6 is considered moderate. A score of 7 to 10 indicates an aggressive tumor.

to the radiation and implant procedures. There would be other elements, as well, which would amount to an overall attack on the problem, including a combination of clinically proven methods that would each separately and together do their part in eradicating the disease.

He explained that the main 'assault' would be a two-pronged attack with radiation. First, I would go through five weeks, of five days per week, of External Beam Therapy. This would be followed, in due course, with a surgical procedure known as Radiation Seed Implantation, an hour-long operation under full or local anesthesia.

But this was not all. Two other cancer-fighting 'weapons' would be called upon. The first was *hormone therapy*. The male hormone known as testosterone, primarily produced by the testicles but also in lesser amounts by the adrenal gland, has been found to aid the growth of prostate tumors. Hence, it is believed controlling testosterone levels may inhibit the growth of such tumors. Hormone therapy involves taking medication which decreases levels of testosterone in the body. Two basic types of hormone drugs achieve this objective: LH-RH analogs and anti-androgen agents.

LH-RH analogs (luterizing hormones) block the production of testosterone by the adrenal gland and testicles, and decrease its presence in the body. They are given by injection only. *Anti-androgen agents* block the adrenal gland from producing testosterone and, to a lesser extent, will inhibit tumor growth. They are taken by mouth and need to be compatible with whatever other drugs are being taken.

Hormonal therapy, which is prescribed for a total of eight months, can cause some discomforting side effects, the principal one being the possibility of slight enlargement of the breasts. Also, the patient may experience 'hot flashes', similar to those of women during menopause.

The second supporting therapy, Dr Gillenwater explained, would be nutritional supplements. These are selected to enhance the body's immune system capabilities and to raise the level of healthy cell formation. The most important of these supplements is an amino acid, but vitamins and trace elements, such as selenium, are also used.

At the conclusion of the meeting with Dr Gillenwater, I was handed a specially-prepared booklet, outlining my entire program and itinerary, customized and calendarized to fit the specific treatments that I was to undergo, over their entire length. It included personal preparation recommendations for each step, a description of what was to be done, and what the effects might be during and after the procedure. It was extremely well-prepared, and left me reassured as to my medical team's organizational efficiency. (I was provided with a graphic chart which was to become my itinerary for the entire program.)

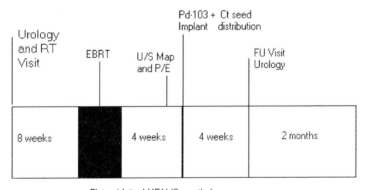

UVA BRACHYTHERAPY PROGRAM
Treatment Protocol High Risk

Urology and RT Visit	EBRT	U/S Map and P/E	Pd-103 + Ct seed Implant distribution	FU Visit Urology
8 weeks		4 weeks	4 weeks	2 months

Flutamide* + LHRH (8 months)

*dose reduced in half in increase of >3 BM's/day. If problem persists, patient will be switched to alternate AA.

RT = Radiation Therapy
EBRT = External Beam Radiation Therapy (5 weeks)
U/S = Ultrasound
P/E = Presurgical Exam
Pd-103 = Palladium-103
FU = Follow Up

When I received my book, I noticed that my program was classified 'High Risk', which made me apprehensive. I immediately asked what this meant. The professor responded that I should not be alarmed by this nomenclature. In essence, it meant that in the hospital's particular system of classifying planned treatments, they were taking no risks and applying every available means to make sure that they would be successful in achieving a complete cure. It was a comforting explanation, which deserves some amplification. The planned protocol was multi-faceted, designed to address my personal situation. Radical Prostatectomy was the invasive approach of cutting out the offending body part, or parts, in a single eradication procedure. Mine was an *all-encompassing* regimen, attacking first and providing support means to bring bodily functions into combative action. My view was that my solution was fully comprehensive, so I gave it a nickname: Radiation Plus!

Armed now with a clear picture of what my decision entailed (Radiation Plus), I took leave of Dr Gillenwater, who graciously expressed his pleasure of having a good, self-educated patient. I proceeded through the labyrinth of corridors to await my next encounter, this time with Professor Rich, head of the Department of Radiation Oncology. A few minutes ensued in the waiting room. With all the inevitable waiting each patient can expect in clinics and hospital lobbies, I suggest one use this time to read and learn more, or contemplate important questions to ask the doctor. This is also a good time to boost one's attitude in a direction of positive-thinking. There were the same magazines, the coffee urn, plastic cups, and the usual accouterments for consumption.

A glance around the waiting room made me realize that cancer has no bounds in whom it strikes, nor where in the body it strikes. There were patients in obvious physical discomfort. Then there were those in wheelchairs, with attendants. There was even a patient receiving oxygen assistance from a portable tank.

Here, I pondered, in a relative sense, how disparate the afflictions are, from critical to optimistically containable and curable. I knew that some of my anonymous waiting room associates were struggling with a much shorter life span than I was. The thought was sobering. My mood became reflective, ranging from the despondency of why I was 'chosen' to be a cancer patient, to determining that even though Fate had dealt me this hand, I was luckier and better off than so many others who had to combat the disease. My resolve to overcome my plight and win my fight was fortified by the professional help I felt assured I was receiving. It was a moment of gathering together all the positive resources and marshaling them to devastate the negative. My mind was set to move forward and overcome!

Eventually, Professor Rich's nurse appeared, clipboard in hand, crisply dressed in the white professional coat I was becoming so familiar with. She announced my name, and I followed her along the aseptic, linoleum corridor to a smaller reception desk, where I checked in. I was politely requested to be weighed. Once this was completed, I was accompanied to an examination room, handed a lightweight green hospital gown, and asked to strip down to my under shorts, to await the arrival of the doctor.

The scene in which I found myself was strictly clinical. The room was dominated by the standard examination table, with two easy chairs to the side. Glass-fronted cabinets, over a stainless steel sink and work area, were cluttered with medical supplies and various instruments. The fluorescent lighting from the ceiling cast a clear, light blue-tinted illumination over the room's stark white walls. The ambiance was cold and sharp. That soon changed when Dr Rich came through the door, together with a second, younger physician, a graduate medical student intern who was assisting him on this particular day. Warm introductions were followed by some general orientation dialogue, a get-to-know-you type of conversation, not limited to health matters.

Dr Rich then conducted a thorough medical examination, while his assistant took notes. At the conclusion, Dr Rich remarked that from the information already in his possession, supplemented by his examination, I was an appropriate candidate for the chosen radiation protocol. He left briefly for me to get dressed.

Soon Dr Rich returned alone. He asked me to make myself comfortable in one of the two easy chairs. He took his place next to me and, with an inviting smile, noted that we would be working closely together for the next months to complete the scheduled protocol. He let me know that he could be reached at *any* time, day or night, should I need him. He proceeded to give me his card, with all the appropriate numbers. He made himself totally available to my needs.

He settled into a full review of the entire program, which was already printed up in my patient booklet. Professor Rich was most accommodating and thorough in answering my questions, as we proceeded. The meeting was over in about forty minutes, at which time I had no doubt that I was on the right path, with the right compassionate professionals, in my resolve *'TO BEAT THIS DISEASE!'*

I had just one final question, 'When do I start?'

Dr Rich answered, 'Today!'

I was directed to report to the Urology Department to have my first hormone therapy shot of Lupron. After receiving my shot, I wandered out to the car, mentally dazed with impressions. I felt very comfortable heading home, my only slight discomfort being the residual sting on my backside from the four-month, slow-release injection of Lupron just administered. As I passed through our nearest township of Lovingston, I stopped at the pharmacy to obtain my second hormone therapy item, a drug called Casodex. This was the anti-androgen medicine that inhibits the minor testosterone production of the adrenal gland. The first step was complete. Now there was an eight-week period of waiting for the hormone treatment to take effect, prior to the commencement of External Beam Radiation.

As the days and weeks passed, I went about life with no changes in my daily routine. Into the third week, I started to experience some 'hot flashes'. Without warning, my whole body would overheat, as though I had walked into a sauna. I would perspire profusely for a few minutes, especially from the head. With the help of a cold, wet facecloth, or the nearest air conditioner going full blast, the flash would abate, amidst much laughter from both my wife and myself. We would take turns flapping each other with newspapers or magazines, when one of us needed relief. What an ironic turn of events!

As time passed, the frequency of hot flashes increased during the day, but included three or four per night. At night, these were unpleasant disruptions of my sleep, which was already being disturbed with increased nightly trips to the bathroom. There were, happily, no signs of the breasts enlarging at any time. I was fortunate not to have experienced any other side effects.

Six weeks into the hormone therapy (two weeks before External Beam Radiation was to begin), I spent a few hours at the Health Services Center getting oriented, educated and prepared for the procedure, so I would 'perform' without resistance. This aspect was handled by the radiologist technician. Great emphasis was placed on special instructions, especially those related to the handling of any side effects, should they occur. A series of X-rays were taken, which were to become critical in directing the radiation beam to the precise treatment area. Indelible markings were painted on my skin in the pelvic, hip, thigh and lower abdominal areas, all of which became targets for lining up the laser beam that would guide the radiating apparatus.

In the preparatory education process, advice was given concerning the short-term side effects of this particular segment of the overall protocol, namely the beam radiation. From this procedure, the pains and discomforts that can occur, but may not, are:

- Skin irritation
- Nausea
- Loss of weight from loss of appetite
- Bladder irritation
- Cramping and loose stool
- Fatigue and loss of energy

The first day of radiation treatment finally arrived, early on a Monday morning. Despite the careful, considerate and complete patient education, it was still a unique initiation experience: materially impressive, yet humanely docile. No pain or discomfort was felt at any time, during the short minutes of radiation exposure.

The beam radiation process should be graphically described, so that a patient is prepared for the visual and sensual impact of the overwhelming dimensions and atmosphere of the scene. It is daunting, but at the same time awe-inspiring, when guided and managed by high-skilled professionals. The first impression upon entering the radiation room is reminiscent of the Death Star command center in *Star Wars*; the difference being that here one is dealing with serious reality, not the imagined!

Upon entering the radiation room, one's first step is to strip down to reveal the target body area, from lower chest to the knees. One is then placed flat, face-up, on a narrow table, and carefully positioned, very exactly, according to electronic control sensors, underneath the platform supporting the body. When correctly positioned, with feet bound in an immovable position, the motorized table slides the patient smoothly, headfirst, in under the radiation apparatus. This is a monstrous machine, which spreads canopy-like over the entire body.

So now the process began. There I was, having been slid through on the table, naked from chest to feet, a target for the radiation miracle of a cancer cure, through shots of intricately aimed beams. A radiation technician supervised the entire activity. He worked with an assistant, who was outside the radiation room, through remote audio and visual means. Before departing the room, just prior to the commencing radiation, the technician advised that with all preparation complete, they would direct the procedure from the outside control panel. I was cautioned to lie motionless, breathing naturally and quietly. When the technician left, the interior lights were dimmed, leaving me in semi-darkness, seeing only various illuminations from control points, and blinking lights denoting electronic activity completing its programmed job. Each beaming is marked only by clicks and radiation machine motor sounds, as the machine rotates to the correct positions for the actual 'shots'. I felt nothing, though indeed powerful things were going on!

The four phases, or beamings, of the programmed radiation 'shoot' were completed in a matter of ten to twelve minutes. The only detectable sensation was the whirring of the machine's movement motor, interspersed with electronic command clicks, setting each change in motion. Despite my apparently vulnerable position, it was all peaceful and painless. I was quietly submissive and absorbed in the technological wonderment happening around me. Then the full lights came on, and the large, radiation-proof door opened. The radiology technician entered and announced that my first beam radiation experience was complete. The automated sliding table moved forward, away from the big apparatus. My feet were untied, and I was helped up. I redressed and departed with a thankful, 'See you tomorrow.'

As I drove home, I reflected seriously upon the marvels of modern medical science. Without having any idea of what the overall future portended, I felt confident again that I was on a positive path, in very competent hands. The hills rolled by, bathed in sunshine, emphasizing the lush green summer colors. Soon I was in my own driveway, going up the hill and to the house. Greeted with anticipation by my wife, I related my experience, and added, 'It was a piece of cake.' No need for more anxiety, no sweat! This was in no way a statement of heroism. It was the simple truth. Calmly and assuredly, I looked forward to the next twenty-four radiation sessions, with no fears of the unknown.

The only apprehension was to await the possible side effects that the radiation process could precipitate. During the patient education sessions, I had learned that not all reactions were the same. Mine in the immediate early stages were mild. During and after the initial sessions, I felt very few effects. I went through the first five sessions with only a loosening stool passage and a slightly more frequent signal rate for urination. My accustomed way of life was little affected. After the fifth or sixth session, I began to feel some lethargy, a general lowering of my energy level. But it did not manifest itself by the need to take any extra bed rest. At most, I simply needed some additional periods in the lounge chair. It was just a lacking inner push to go out and do this or that, in response to my habitual compulsion to expend energy. Those motivations were still met, and the jobs were completed.

Probably the most intrusive personal sensation was that my normally hearty appetite diminished. Food just did not taste the same. Something was inexplicably different. As it turned out, I lost some weight, despite the good food being provided. My appetite simply disappeared. Was it metabolic change? Most likely, it was a side effect from the radiation.

The next five weeks became quite routine. I departed from home early every morning for my radiation appointments. With an hour commute each way, I was usually home by midday, with the rest of the day available for my own activities. So far, everything seemed to be going as planned.

IV

By the middle of the twenty-five session beam radiation routine, there were combinations of effects caused by the various incursions into and upon my body. Here are the aggregate effects I experienced as the treatments wore on through their planned process:

Hormonal Treatment. The hot flashes intensified per occurrence, meaning an increased profusion of heat and sweat. The most irritating were the five to six flashes that now occurred at night while I slept. Also, my breasts became sensitive and tender, with mild pain—though thankfully there was no perceptible growth in size. The genitals diminished slowly in mass, and became permanently limp and sexually decommissioned. However, my libido itself was unaltered. Perhaps it was all illusory, a question of a physiological shut-down, accompanied by no perceptible psychological change. It seemed that desire and consequent attraction remained natural. I discussed this paradox with Dr Rich in one of my weekly meetings. He noted it in the record, and cursorily commented that my reaction was unique for patients in his care undergoing similar protocols.

Beam Radiation. Taking into account that this procedure took five weeks, with five episodes per week, my body's signals were based on an accumulative effect regimen. As already stated, in the first three weeks, fifteen radiation sessions caused very mild reactions, in my case. As the final ten sessions were nearing completion, however, there was some intensification in side effects. These were within the parameters of the forewarnings which I had been given:

33

- Skin irritation was not experienced at all (although extremely common for most).
- Nausea was common.
- Loss of appetite was moderate, but apparent.
- Bladder irritation was very evident, manifest in greatly increased signals of need for voiding, accompanied by an inability to empty the bladder entirely per movement. This caused a continuous feeling of having to urinate, and a fear that I might not be able to control the bladder. It was very annoying. Nightly, sleep interruptions were frequent, and growing in number, which was frustrating. These interruptions also created an apprehension that I was not acquiring adequate, healthy rest. I sensed a fear of overall debilitation.
- Bowel function was impaired by a confusing sensation, perhaps related to the bladder irritation, which caused a frequent, mostly false, sensation of the need to have a movement. This was particularly odious to the extent that I never knew if the signal was real or not! Then, of course, it was a gamble, but I took no risks—many frustrated runs to the nearest facility. Thankfully no accidents were recorded! It was, however, stressful. Of my genuine bowel movements, these were always loose, a condition which continued through the entire treatment process.
- Fatigue occurred in a moderate sense. As mentioned, there was an overall lessened desire to undertake activities that required physical effort. As a fervent tennis player, I found the very idea of picking up a racquet unattractive. Certain domestic activities in the home and in the yard were comfortably pursuable, though, such as watering my garden. While the fatigue factor grew, sleeping was desired, though not always satisfying during the night hours. My multiple bathroom visits

did interfere with my overall rest, but eventually, after each episode, I was able to resume my sleep pattern.

- Both my mind and spirit were in a positive mode, considering all that was happening. The knowledge of how well the entire program and protocol had been prepared was a soothing reassurance that I would and could *BEAT THIS DISEASE!* There were, of course, fears of whether it would work in its finality. But my belief was: have faith, remain determined, and it will happen! When I did, at times, slip into periods of doubt and fear, my inherent optimism and will to succeed eventually prevailed, dispelling the darker thoughts and fears.

During the beam radiation process, everything went much as expected. But there were several deviations and exceptions. No matter what is predicted during treatment, one can count on something unexpected to cause a frightening experience. About halfway through my beam radiation treatments, I went to bed one evening and woke up after only a few hours with a feverish feeling and intense nausea. Shortly thereafter I felt the need to vomit, and I rushed to the bathroom. I returned to bed, hoping for a continued night of peaceful sleep. But my body had other plans. The shivers of fever increased. I couldn't keep warm; I couldn't stay cool. Soon the pressures of an intense, impelling bowel movement sent me running to the bathroom again.

Mentally, I was getting agitated and nervous. *What's happening here?! Did they miscalculate and give me an overdose of radiation today?* While these thoughts were circulating in my mind, my discomfort persisted. I spent the rest of the night sleepless, with fever, cramps, nausea and no rest. By 5 a.m., I had reached my limits, so I decided to get up and phone Dr Rich on the 'on-call' number he had given me. I did so, and within forty minutes, he called back. I explained my predicament. He told me to be at his clinic at 11 a.m. I was relieved to have such an immediate response!

My morning continued with all the same symptoms that I had experienced during the night. No appetite for breakfast. I had some dried toast and a dose of Pepto Bismol, which seemed to quiet things down a little. At 10 a.m., I was out the door and on my way to see Dr Rich. He was at his alternative clinic, which appeared to be a post-operative facility. He gave me a thorough examination. He took a careful look at all the current clinical findings and concluded that my situation was unlikely to be related to my treatment. He thought I was dealing with a separate infection, such as gastrointestinal flu. He prescribed several basic remedial actions, suggested rest, plenty of liquids, Tylenol for the fever, then sent me back home with the request that I call any time—but especially if my condition had not improved dramatically in the following twenty-four hours. I followed his script and within a day the whole problem had subsided. I did, however, continue to feel listless and fatigued for several days.

The importance of this event is really only to emphasize that, while the obsession and concentration is on the main cancer treatment itself, it is important to realize that exposure to other maladies, with their own symptoms and discomforts, may still occur and perhaps mislead a patient in terms of unnecessary worry.

The external radiation procedure continued with no perceptible variations, until finally the twenty-fifth and final session was completed. It was a happy day of relief when I walked out of the Radiology Department knowing that this phase of the protocol was behind me. Adding to my enjoyment during the ride home was knowing that I was now scheduled for three weeks without any treatments. For one, I was relieved not to have the two-hour daily commute between my country home and Charlottesville. It was a welcome time of rest and recuperation. I was going to make the best of it!

My overall feeling of fatigue continued to grow, however, and my energy level subsided further. Tiredness in the evening was often oppressive, and the desire to retire to bed came earlier and heavier, as the days progressed. Nights continued to be interrupted with multiple awakenings, by the sensation to void, interspersed with nausea, and at times, bowel movements. So it was not always restful, but there was some release from mental pressure, in the sense that these side effects were 'normal', an expected consequence of the beam radiation.

About ten days prior to seed implant surgery, a critically important procedure had to be completed, called Ultrasound Mapping. *Ultrasound Mapping* is a process which is critical to the ability of the surgeons to successfully conduct the radioactive seed implantation. With the use of ultrasound technology, images are created that measure the volume of the prostate gland and the pubic arch, and confirm the size and exact location of the tumor. From this information, the surgeons can calculate the number of seeds to be implanted. They will, furthermore, be provided with a graphic on-screen 'blueprint' to guide them through the placement procedure, when surgery is conducted.

Once in the ultrasound room, one is stripped from the waist down and laid, back-down, on an examination table. One's legs are in the 'lithotomic' position, placed in obstetric-gynecological stirrups. A catheter is inserted through the penis, which allows for identification of *prostatic urethra*. The catheter serves the dual purpose of allowing continued free-flow of urine, but also provides guidance images for essential areas. When satisfactory positioning has been achieved, an ultrasound probe is inserted through the rectum. Correctly placed, it will transmit a series of detailed images, providing information on the volume and exact positioning of the tumor in the prostate. This way, the radiation oncologist, through analysis of the images made, will provide the surgeons with a blueprint, or map, of exactly how to proceed with implantation in the operating room.

Once the mapping is complete, there is a final step in the surgery preparation program. I was escorted to an examination room for a general physical examination, completed by a practitioner nurse. It is basically a repeat of the process at the inception of the entire treatment: blood sampling for analysis, pulse and blood pressure measurements, check of any changes in body performance, listing of prescription drugs being taken, check of weight, and any other variations of well-being that might have occurred during the most recent month. I was then asked, after a detailed explanation, which form of anesthesia I would prefer, from spinal block (under which one is aware of all the proceedings), to total (which renders you completely unconscious). I chose the latter. This completed, I breathed another sigh of relief and headed out to my car for the trip home. I found myself in a contented, peaceful frame of mind, concluding that most of the steps of the treatment path were now successfully behind me.

Implantation surgery was to take place nine days later. I made my best effort to enjoy these days without medical appointments, and resumed my daily routine of activity. I even took a three-day trip to visit my son and his family in North Carolina. I did discover, during this trip, that sitting in an automobile for a prolonged period of time was distinctly uncomfortable. Such immobility constantly gave me strong sensations of having to void the bladder. Unfortunately, despite several stops on the roadside to run for the bushes, an inability to complete total voiding caused continuous discomfort. My anxiety grew as we approached Charlotte. We were now surrounded by semi-developed areas, and I had fewer opportunities to stop and get partial relief at the roadside! We were going to celebrate our son's fortieth birthday, and I wanted to arrive in good spirits, showing no signs of the stress which my ordeal was placing on me. The effort to make the occasion a joyous one was worthwhile, and the weekend was a successful family reunion.

Upon returning home, I followed a 'normal' daily regimen, attending to the administrative needs of our farm. There was, naturally, time for leisure activities, reading, enjoying the outdoors, catching radio and TV programs. While my state of mind was mostly tranquil, I had reached a point of being anxious to complete the program and have the entire treatment behind me. While my belief in its success was unwavering, the prospect of its conclusion was highly desired. Maybe I was just getting a little combat-fatigued, with the end of the 'war' in sight. The days seemed almost endless, and crept by at a petty pace. Finally, I reached the day when I needed to prepare myself for surgery.

I precisely followed my written instructions, commencing with steps to be taken up to the twenty-four hours before surgery. These were:

1. Start prescribed antibiotic (preventive measure) at midday, on the day before surgery was scheduled.

2. At 4 p.m., start clear liquid diet.

3. At 4 p.m., drink one bottle (8 oz.) of magnesium citrate.

4. At 8 p.m., administer one Fleets enema.

5. After midnight, no solid foods to be taken. May consume clear liquids until one hour prior to surgery.

6. On the morning of surgery, administer an additional Fleets enema.

7. May take regular medication, unless otherwise instructed.

8. May not take aspirin or ibuprofen medication for one week prior to surgery. (If taking blood-thinning medication, consult physician. Pre-existing heart, vascular and lung conditions must also be brought to the attention of the attending physician.)

Having completed all of the mandated preparations, I was finally ready early on the appointed morning. Because it was strictly prohibited for a patient to drive home following the out-patient surgery, my wife accompanied me to the health center for the first time. She came with me into the waiting area. We arrived two hours prior to surgery. Once again, more waiting room time! The difference now was that I was in a room designated for patients going into surgery. It was eerily quiet.

I cast my eyes around, looking at each of the occupants. It was not a cheerful scene, glum to the point of morbidity. I took solace in the hope and belief that I was blessed; destined to rid myself of my disease, because of the expertise of the very competent physicians to whom I had entrusted my fate. I hoped that those surrounding me would be as fortunate as I expected to be. No sooner had I started scanning the day's *Washington Post*, than I was called to the reception desk. I knew now that I was embarked on the final and crucial phase. My wife's parting words wishing me good luck flashed through my mind.

A surgical nurse accompanied me to a nearby preparation room, which was dominated by an ambulant hospital bed table. This was surrounded by the usual facilities in stainless steel, interspersed by a profusion of medical apparatus. I was left to disrobe and don the lightweight green hospital gown, then asked to lie down on the table bed. Soon the nurse returned to commence my final pre-surgical examination: blood pressure and pulse; a check on all vital functions; questions on whether I had followed all preparatory procedures, and whether I had any special discomforts or side effects through all the completed stages of treatment. It was very thorough and competently precise.

She was in possession of the results of my most recent blood work, which she said were very good. Most dramatic of these results was that my PSA count was down to 0.1, as a result of the treatments already completed. I was elated!

Soon I was being propelled by a hospital orderly, trundled out of the first prep room, on what seemed an endless trip. I watched the lights and the ceiling go by, until I was in the final surgical preparation room, a large area divided into sections by flimsy white curtains running along stainless steel ceiling rails. I was parked in my separate enclosed section, provided with an identification bracelet and connected to an intravenous flow. My next visitor introduced himself as my anesthesiologist and checked that, in fact, I had chosen general anesthesia, which I confirmed. Having been given preparatory sedation, I was already relaxed and drowsy. I remember being given an injection, and from that point on, nothingness.

The next thing I recall was regaining consciousness under the same perceived circumstances, surrounded by white curtains. I slowly focused on the ceiling. It was a calm, pleasant experience. For a moment, I was confused as to whether surgery was yet to begin, or whether it was in fact completed. Reality crept back at a slow pace, and in time I knew it was all done and over. I was drowsily contented, as the world was returning to me once again!

Between visits from the recovery area nurses, I dozed off, but realized I was gradually gaining fuller consciousness. Finally I was asked to get up and dress, after disconnection from my intravenous line. It was only then that I noticed the catheter and the receptacle bag that had been strapped to my leg below the knee. It was to remain in place until natural voiding returned. I was just about to get dressed when my wife arrived, in the company of Dr Gillenwater and Dr Rich, who had together performed the implant surgery. In my still fuzzy state, my wife's and their familiar faces were a welcome sight.

The two doctors informed me that the entire procedure had been completed satisfactorily, and they were pleased with the result. After a series of tests of my vital functions, I was free to get fully clothed (with the help of my wife), and to head out of the hospital, returning home to rest and recuperate. A floating sense of relief ensued! On the trip home, I nodded off intermittently, providing little companionship for my wife. With a combination of the residual effect of the anesthesia wearing off, and the pain-relievers I had been given, there was a little discomfort, but no real pain. I spent the balance of the afternoon and evening resting in bed, dozing off and on, between short periods of clear awareness. As night fell, deeper sleep ensued.

It was not until dawn broke that clearer sensations began slowly returning. There was stiffness and pain in the area of the scrotum and rectum, and also in the upper legs and the thigh area. No acute internal pain was felt in the target area where the implants had been placed. There was just a dull aching. As the day wore on, it became clear that there was no bleeding beneath the scrotum, nor was blood being passed in the urine. Though there was swelling and tenderness in the area between the legs, all of the after-effects were mild when compared to the forewarnings of what one could possibly expect.

Nevertheless, I made the decision to take it easy, and spent the first forty-eight hours with a minimal amount of activity or movement, most of the time in a comfortable easy chair, propped up by cushions placed to provide pressure relief to critical sensitive areas. Keeping my legs up on an ottoman stool was a great help. Short strolls through the house and outside provided stimulation to blood circulation and relief from sedentary inactivity.

Two full days after the implant surgery, I was back at the Health Services Center. I was to have a bladder evacuation test, to determine whether the catheter could be removed. The test was affirmative and its removal completed, but not without acrid pain. A quick 'look-over' examination by Dr

Gillenwater produced a satisfactory conclusion, with everything being pronounced in good shape. I was happily free to return home, where I resumed my daily routine and way of living, albeit in a somewhat quieter way than usual.

Several side effects persisted for a few days, such as overly frequent urination, accompanied by a burning sensation when passing water, and that continuous sense of urgency to urinate. These were somewhat tedious irritations. General swelling and bruising of the scrotum area lasted only ten days and caused very little in the way of problems or discomfort. The return to my more active lifestyle was soon achieved, and I was on my way, feeling gratified, if not totally unburdened.

Often I thought to myself throughout the day: *I THINK WE'RE BEATING THIS DISEASE! AT LEAST IT SEEMS LIKE IT NOW!*

This may be a time to address the aspects of influence on sexual behavior, whether psychological or physiological. These are side effects of a very sensitive and personal nature, and are, to a certain extent, private. They are also unique to each individual as they occur.

My experience was one of consternation and subsequent confusion. It was a paradox of a healthy sexual state of mind, contrasted with a neutralized ability. My libido remained constant, if not in fact augmented. Perhaps this was the male psyche, fearing the loss of its power of potency. Perhaps it was a case of overreacting to the threat of becoming impotent. The natural drive to prove that I could still attract the opposite sex became almost obsessive.

The enigmatic conclusion of the effects on sexual reaction, in my case, remains unanswered. It can best be described as a profusion of confusion. Perhaps enough has been said. Each of us has to deal with what we perceive and can do. My experience has thus far been inconclusive, frustrating and enigmatic. However, what remains, thankfully, is my recovery and general state of good health.

V

Four weeks after the implant surgery, I was back at the health center for another follow-up visit with Drs Gillenwater and Rich. They wanted to check my healing condition for any possible variations from the norm, as well as conduct an assessment of my general well-being. The regular clinical tests and physical inspections were carried out. Fortunately, the results were deemed satisfactory. This was a wonderful affirmation that mine was a normal recovery, perhaps even a mild one.

A further check-up two months later revealed nothing of consequence, and I was asked if I would return for a diagnostic and general health visit six months hence. Meantime, I continued on the prescribed amino acid and vitamin supplement program. My physical well-being continued to improve to a point where I felt that I had regained my own strength and energy. How else can I put it: I felt good! I was enjoying the gradual steady improvement as time passed.

The whole regimen, from diagnosis to completion of the selected curative program, so carefully and professionally carried out over six months, was now successfully concluded. Gratitude and relief were—and still are—my foremost feelings.

I have documented my experience in order to share knowledge about the successful treatment of prostrate cancer with others similarly afflicted. My intention is to provide guidance in understanding the illness, and pass on the belief that a cure *is* achievable! In conclusion, I must give great credit to those of the medical profession who, through tenacious and dedicated work, continue to advance the cause of defining cancer and finding its cure. In my particular case, the Departments of Urology and Radiation Oncology at the University of Virginia Health System stand out with their eminent scientific achievements. I will be forever grateful to the men and women involved in these priceless endeavors!

Life Goes On

Two years have passed since the fateful moment when I learned the news of my original diagnosis. The protocols and treatments completed, described in the foregoing pages, fortunately leave me living the life that was mine before this 'interlude'. The only difference is that now there are certain disciplines being routinely followed, which are simply supportive of a general desire to stay healthy, given the knowledge gained through the entire process of being cured of prostate cancer.

Stimulating the individual's immune system to combat a disease is a major objective of scientific research. How do you stimulate the body to put its defense mechanisms to work?

I have given this aspect of my fight against prostate cancer a great deal of thought, in regard to how it might have helped me to be cured. This is why!

I was born in Malaysia in 1931 and grew up to the age of ten in the primitive country conditions that prevailed. In those early formative years I endured a number of tropical diseases, with scant, crude medical help. The infections included two bouts of malaria, amebic dysentery, dengue fever and a host of minor tropical afflictions, beyond the 'normal' childhood diseases.

Could this early exposure to these afflictions, which the body's inherent combative immune system overcame—barely, at one point— have created a stronger resistance to disease capability? Maybe, maybe not. I choose to believe it helped in the defeat of my prostate cancer affliction.

So life goes on! With the help of advanced medical professionalism, in its specific area of expertise, I so far have been fortunate enough to 'beat this disease'! The question remains of how to keep free of cancer's recurrence, in the way one lives. So life will go on in a slightly altered way, forever.

One must remain intensely watchful and alert. So this is what one, with varying advice, should beneficially attempt to do.

The most important routine to follow is in the sphere of vigilance: checkups. One should be subjected to medical examination, with one's urologist and oncology/radiation physicians, every three months during the first year after the completion of the treatment protocol. This requires blood work preceding each appointment. Particularly important from the analysis results, is to arrive at the crucial PSA number. In terms of vigilance, it is advisable that checkups also be completed by one's family doctor or internist, at least once every six months during the first year following the completion of one's treatment. This is important because a family doctor monitors general health, beyond what the specialist physicians are responsible for, in terms of one's completed prostate treatment. There are many varied physical aspects to one's well-being that always need to be watched.

It would also be advisable to ask for certain examinations that reach beyond the call of a routine general medical checkup. In my case, I requested a complete colonoscopy—since the colon is in the general area of where my cancer occurred. It is a fairly common cancer area, to begin with. Make sure you get it checked, too!

The human body's functions have many facets, all of which are interrelated. The treatment of prostate cancer, or for that matter, any form of cancer, throws certain of these functions temporarily out of balance, owing to the nature of the invasive physical incursions that have occurred. As complete health is restored, the wondrous process of recovery and re-balancing will occur naturally. This return to normality can and should be aided in different ways.

The nutritional supplement regimen followed during the treatment period should be continued following its successful completion. For prostate cancer recovery, amounts of the aforementioned L-Arginine Freeform amino acid, selenium, and zinc tablets are recommended on a daily basis, along with the other dietary supplements, vitamins and minerals.

The whole experience has also had its traumatic effects beyond just the body. An element of psychological impact has been experienced. If there are lasting effects of the emotional experience, continuing apprehension, doubts and the like, psychological help should be sought.

Such help may be sought from a number of cancer patient support groups. These fellowships are to be found in different parts of the country. They provide group therapy assistance in the form of roundtable meetings, lectures and discussions, which are most commonly conducted by a professional, be it physician or psychologist. Many publish newsletters to disseminate general information, or give specific advice on cancer-related problems.

Membership is inexpensive and encompasses patients under treatment, as well as those already recovered. Some better known groups are: USTOO, Man to Man and PAACT. They may be found on the Internet, or by asking one's physician. One such group situated in Charlottesville, Virginia, is called 'The Prostate Forum', and was founded by Professor Charles E. Meyers, former director of the University of Virginia Cancer Center. He is himself a survivor of prostate cancer. He continues to take an active part in leading this organization.

Epilogue

Most still get prostate cancer,
comes with age and
it's nothing you catch.

Thirty years ago I was taught to finger feel
for firmness and nodules.
Today it's numbers and needles.
PSA?
Mine's three; what's yours? Seven?
Think you should have a biopsy.

Now they come
into the clinic armed from the Internet,
but not knowing.
Who will they see,
What will they feel,
What do they know,
for sure?

Your cancer can be cured
by irradiation and hormones
which kill the cancer.
The beams are aimed
the seeds are inserted.
Let the shooting begin.

To push the treatment beyond
the technical,
the mechanisms,
even the professional,
do one thing:

Listen to the patient!

Tyvin A. Rich, MD
Professor, Radiation Oncology

Glossary

Abdomen: The part of the body located below the ribs and above the pelvic bone.

Adjuvant therapy: A treatment method used in addition to the primary therapy. Radiation therapy is often used as an adjuvant to surgery;

Adrenal glands: Two glands located above the kidneys (one above each kidney). They produce several kinds of hormones, including a small amount of sex hormones.

Androgens: Male sex hormones produced by the testicles and, in small amounts, by the adrenal glands.

Anesthesia: Loss of feeling or sensation resulting from the use of certain drugs or gases.

Angiogenesis: The formation of new blood vessels.

Antiangiogenesis: Preventing the development of new blood vessels.

Anus: The opening at the lower end of the rectum through which solid waste is eliminated.

Benign: A nonmalignant or noncancerous condition.

Benign Prostatic Hyperplasia/Benign Prostatic Hypertrophy (BPH):   A noncancerous, yet serious condition of the prostate; generally, an enlargement of the gland, causing obstruction of urination, which can result in secondary complications.

Bilateral Orchiectomy: Surgical removal of the testicles to halt production of testosterone.

Biopsy: The procedure to obtain tissue, which is then examined by a pathologist using a microscope to distinguish between cancerous and noncancerous conditions; for prostate cancer this may be a needle biopsy, or transurectal resection of the prostate (TUR/P).

Bladder: The hollow organ that stores urine.

Blood chemistry: Analysis of multiple components in the serum (blood), including tests to evaluate function of the liver and kidneys, minerals, cholesterol, etc.; important especially because abnormal values can indicate spread of cancer, or side effects of treatment(s).

Blood count: Analysis, primarily of red blood cells (which help transport oxygen in the body), white blood cells (which protect against infection), and platelets (necessary for clotting of blood); abnormal values can indicate cancerous involvement of the bone marrow, or side effects of the treatment(s).

Brachytherapy: Treatment with radioactive sources placed into or very near the tumor in the affected area; includes surface application, body cavity application, and placement into the tissue. Sometimes this term is used interchangeably with 'internal radiation therapy'.

CT scan (Computerized Tomography): A computer-assisted type of X-ray, allowing detailed visualization of the body; particularly useful in evaluating soft-tissue organs.

Cancer: A general term for more than 100 diseases in which abnormal cells multiply without control. Cancer cells can spread through the bloodstream and lymphatic system to the other parts of the body.

Castration: Elimination of testicular function, either by surgical removal of the testes (surgical castration), or by administration of an LHRH analog (a class of drugs designed to inhibit testicular function).

Carcinoma: Cancer that begins in the lining or covering of an organ.

Catheterization: Inserting a catheter through the urethra into the bladder.

Chemotherapy: Treatment with anticancer drugs.

Clinical trials: Studies conducted with patients, usually to evaluate a promising new drug or treatment. Each study is designed to answer scientific questions and find better ways to treat patients.

Cobalt 60: A radioactive substance used as a radiation source to treat cancer.

Cystoscope: A lighted instrument used to look at the inside of the bladder.

Diagnosis: Evaluation of symptoms and/or tests leading to the verification of the existence of an abnormal condition.

Diploid: Slow-growing prostate cancer cells.

Ejaculation: The release of semen through the penis during orgasm.

Estrogen: A female sex hormone.

External radiation therapy: Treatment with high energy radiation given from a source located outside the body.

Flow Cytometry: The process by which graphs or histograms are plotted based on the DNA content of the cancerous tissue cells.

Foley Catheter: In terms of men, a foley catheter is a tube that is inserted through the tip of the penis into the urethra until it enters the bladder.

Hormone: A chemical substance that is formed in one part of the body, travels through the blood, and affects the function of cells elsewhere in the body.

Hormone therapy: Treatment that prevents cancer cells from getting the hormones they need to grow. Hormone therapy for prostate cancer keeps the cancer cells from getting male hormones. Treatment may involve removing the testicles or giving female hormones or other drugs to prevent the production of male hormones or to block their effect on cancer cells.

Hyperthermia: Using heat produced by microwave radiation to treat prostate cancer.

Implant: A small container of radioactive material placed in or near a cancer.

Impotence: Partial or complete loss of erection, which may be associated with a loss of libido; may be a result of injury secondary to radiation therapy or surgical resection of the prostate, which may or may not be permanent or may be a result of hormone deprivation therapy.

Incision: A cut made during surgery.

Incontinence: Partial or complete loss of urine control; may be a result of injury secondary to radiation therapy or surgical resection of the prostate.

Internal radiation: A type of therapy in which a radioactive substance is implanted into or close to the area needing treatment.

Interstitial implant: A radioactive source placed directly into the tissue (not in a body cavity).

Intravenous pyelogram: X-rays of the kidneys, ureters, and bladder taken after a dye is injected into a vein. Also called IVP.

Linear accelerator: A machine that creates high energy radiation to treat cancers using electricity to form a stream of fast moving subatomic particles.

Local therapy: Treatment that affects a tumor and tissue near it.

Luteinizing hormone-releasing hormone: A hormone that controls sex hormones in men and women. Also called LHRH.

Luteinizing hormone-releasing hormone (LHRH) agonist: A substance that closely resembles LHRH, which controls the production of sex hormones. However, LHRH agonists affect the body differently than does LHRH. LHRH agonists keep the testicles from producing hormones.

Lymph: The almost colorless fluid that travels through the lymphatic system and carries cells that help fight infection

Lymph nodes: Small, bean-shaped organs located along the channels of the lymphatic system. The lymph nodes store special cells that can trap bacteria or cancer cells traveling through the body in lymph nodes. Also called lymph glands.

Lymphadenectomy: The surgical removal of one or more lymph nodes for purposes of microscopic examination; may be performed as an 'open pelvic lymphadenectomy' as the initial approach during radical prostatectomy, or a separate procedure prior to radical prostatectomy by means of small incision(s) into the pelvic cavity ('laparoscopic lymphadenectomy').

Lymphatic system: The tissues and organs that produce, store, and carry cells that fight infection and disease. This system includes the bone marrow, spleen, thymus, lymph nodes, and channels that carry lymph.

MRI (Magnetic Resonance Imaging) scan: A sophisticated use of an electromagnet and sound waves to create a detailed X-ray type image by measurement of signal intensity of a particular body part or region; in general, this may be the most effective means of detecting whether the tumor has penetrated through the capsule of the prostate gland and/or invaded the seminal vesicle(s), and can be used to evaluate whether pelvic lymph nodes are enlarged.

Malignant;:   Cancerous; can spread to other parts of the body.

Metastasis: (plural is metastases): Spread or transfer of a malignant tumor to another part of the body not directly connected to the original tumor location; all malignant (cancerous) tumors have the potential to metastasize (spread), while benign conditions do not.

Moderately Differentiated: A classification of prostate cancer in which the cells are beginning to lose their shape and is graded between 5 and 8.

Oncologist: A doctor who specializes in treating cancer. Some oncologists specialize in a particular type of cancer treatment. For example, a radiation oncologist treats cancer with radiation.

Orchiectomy: Surgery to remove the testicles.

Palliative therapy: A treatment that may relieve symptoms without curing the disease.

Pathologist: A doctor who identifies disease by studying cells and tissues under a microscope.

Pelvic: Referring to the area of the body located at below the waist and surrounded by the hip and pubic bones.

Perineal prostatectomy: Surgery to remove the prostate through an incision made between the scrotum and the anus.

Poorly Differentiated: A late classification of prostate cancer in which there is no definite shape of the cells which is graded between 9 and 10.

Primary: A term that refers to the organ, gland, etc., where the cancer begins, from which it may then spread (for example, 'primary' prostate cancer which may 'metastasize' to the bone).

Prognosis: The probable outcome or course of a disease; the chance of recovery.

Progression: A term used to describe continued growth of the cancer, or recurrence of cancer after a previous response to treatment.

Prostate: A male sex gland; it produces a fluid that forms part of semen.

Prostate acid phosphatase: An enzyme produced by the prostate that is elevated in some patients with prostate cancer.

Prostate-specific antigen: A protein whose level in the blood goes up in some men who have prostate cancer or benign prostatic hyperplasia. Also called PSA.

Prostate Specific Antigen (PSA) Assay: A blood test for the measurement of a substance produced by prostate gland cells; used both for screening (an elevation of the PSA indicates an abnormal condition of the prostate gland, either benign or malignant, requiring further investigation for diagnosis), and to monitor the progress of a patient undergoing treatment and/or after surgery or radiation therapy; it is the most sensitive 'marker' of prostate cancer that is currently available.

Prostatectomy: An operation to remove part or all of the prostate.

Prostate acid phosphatase: An enzyme produced by the prostate. Its level in the blood goes up in some men who have prostate cancer. Also called PAP.

Prostatic Acid Phosphatase (PAP) Assay: A blood test to measure a substance most notably (not exclusively) produced by prostate gland cells; also useful as a 'marker' because the PAP is typically elevated if there is metastasis.

Rad: Short form for 'radiation absorbed dose'; a measurement of the amount of radiation absorbed by tissues (100 rad = 1 gray).

Radiation: Energy carried by waves or a stream of particles.

Radiation therapy: Treatment with high energy rays from X-rays or other sources to damage cancer cells. The radiation may come from a machine (external radiation therapy) or from radioactive materials placed inside the body as close as possible to the cancer (internal radiation therapy).

Radiaton Oncologist: A physician with special training in reading diagnostic X-rays and performing specialized X-ray procedures

Radiation physicist A person trained to ensure that the radiation machine delivers the right amount of radiation to the treatment site.

Radical prostatectomy: Surgery to remove the entire prostate. The two types of radical prostatectomy are retropubic prostatectomy and perineal prostatectomy.

Radiotherapy: See radiation therapy.

Rectal exam: A procedure in which a doctor inserts a gloved, lubricated finger into the rectum and feels the prostate through the wall of the rectum to check the prostate for hard or lumpy areas.

Refractory: A term used most commonly to describe the situation when the disease is no longer controlled by current therapy; similar to 'progression'.

Remission: Disappearance of the signs and symptoms of cancer. When this happens, the disease is said to be 'in remission'. Remission can be temporary or permanent.

Response: A decrease in the extent of disease as evidenced by reduction or disappearance of visible tumor and/or markers, which may be complete or partial; because untreated cancers are generally progressive, stability (no change) of disease is sometimes considered to be a positive response to treatment.

Retropubic prostatectomy: Surgical removal of the prostate through an incision in the abdomen.

Scrotum: The external pouch of skin that contains the testicles.

Semen: The fluid that is released through the penis during orgasm. Semen is made up of sperm from the testicles and fluid from the prostate and other sex glands.

Simulation: A process involving special X-ray pictures that are used to plan radiation treatment so the areas to be treated are precisely located and marked for treatment.

Stage: A categorical assessment of the degree to which a cancer has grown at the time of initial diagnosis or at a point of reevaluation; a very simple implication is that the more advanced the stage of disease may be, there is greater likelihood that the disease represents a potentially fatal illness.

Staging: The actual process of categorically assessing the extent of prostate cancer.

TRUS-P (Transrectal Ultrasound of the Prostate): A test using soundwave echoes to create an image of an organ or gland to visually inspect for abnormal conditions; helpful in assessing the prostate gland for enlargement, nodules, and penetration of the tumor through the capsule of the gland and/or invasion of the seminal vesicle(s); extremely useful for guidance of needle biopsies of the prostate gland.

TURIP (Transurectal Resection of the Prostate): A surgical procedure by which small portions of the prostate gland are removed through incision of the inside of the urethra (through the penis); a TUR/P is often performed to relieve obstruction of urine flow because of compression of urethra due to enlargement of the prostate; many times unsuspected cancer is discovered in the resected specimen when this procedure is done for presumed benign enlargement of the prostate gland.

Testicles: The two egg-shaped glands that produce sperm and male hormones.

Testosterone: A male sex hormone.

Transurethral resection: The use of a special instrument inserted through the penis to remove a small prostate tumor. This procedure can also be accomplished by laser.

Tumor: An abnormal mass of tissue. Tumors are either benign or malignant.

Ultrasound: A technique that uses sound waves that cannot be heard by humans to produce pictures of areas inside the body. The pictures are created by a computer that analyzes the echoes produced by the waves as they bounce off tissues.

Ureter: The tube that carries urine from each kidney to the bladder.

Urethra: The tube that carries urine or semen to the outside of the body.

Urologist: A doctor who specializes in diseases of the urinary organs in females and the urinary and sex organs in males.

Well-differentiated: An early classification of prostate cancer in which the cells have definite shape which is graded between 1 and 4.

X-ray: High energy radiation that can be used at low levels to diagnose disease or at high levels to treat cancer.